For Amy, John, and Matthew
—L.C.

To Lucille Colandro, whose stories spark my imagination.
—J.L.

ISBN 978-1-338-66840-7
10 9 8 7 6 5 4 3 2 1   22 23 24 25 26
Printed in the U.S.A. 61 • First edition, January 2022

THERE WAS AN OLD SCIENTIST WHO SWALLOWED A DINOSAUR!

by Lucille Colandro

illustrated by Jared Lee

Cartwheel Books

an imprint of Scholastic Inc.

There was an old scientist who swallowed a dinosaur.
I don't know why she swallowed a dinosaur,
but she went to explore.

There was an old scientist who swallowed a fern.
It was her turn to swallow a fern.

She swallowed the fern to feed the dinosaur.

I don't know why she swallowed a dinosaur,
but she went to explore.

There was an old scientist who swallowed a rock.
Just a chip off the block to swallow that rock.

She swallowed the rock to weigh down the fern.

She swallowed the fern to feed the dinosaur.

I don't know why she swallowed a dinosaur,

but she went to explore.

23

There was an old scientist who
swallowed a pick.

She knew it wouldn't stick
when she swallowed that pick.

She swallowed the pick to examine the rock.
She swallowed the rock to weigh down the fern.

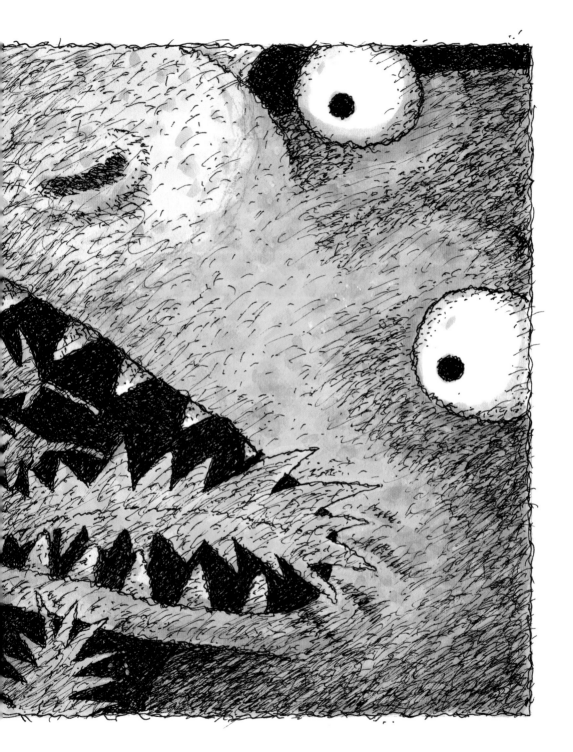

She swallowed the fern to feed the dinosaur.

I don't know why she swallowed a dinosaur,

but she went to explore.

There was an old scientist who
swallowed a dustpan.
It was part of her plan to swallow the dustpan.

She swallowed the dustpan to clean the pick.
She swallowed the pick to examine the rock.

She swallowed the rock to weigh down the fern.

She swallowed the fern to feed the dinosaur.

I don't know why she swallowed a dinosaur,
but she went to explore.

There was an old scientist who
swallowed a sifting screen.
To keep the fossils clean, she
swallowed that screen.

She swallowed the screen to fill the dustpan.
She swallowed the pan to clean the pick.

She swallowed the pick to examine the rock.
She swallowed the rock to weigh down the fern.

She swallowed the fern to feed the dinosaur.

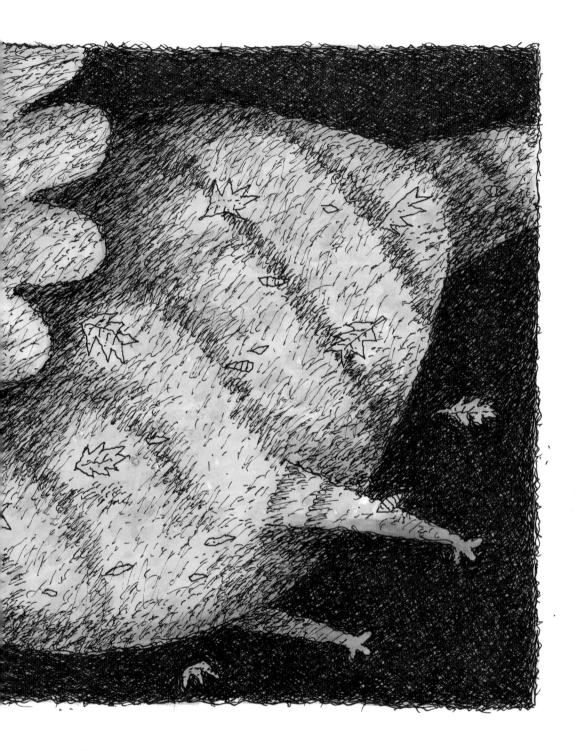

I don't know why she swallowed a dinosaur,
but she went to explore.

A hammer, chisels, and brushes are part of the tool kit.

There was an old scientist who swallowed a pen.
To keep track of where, how, and when,
she swallowed that pen.

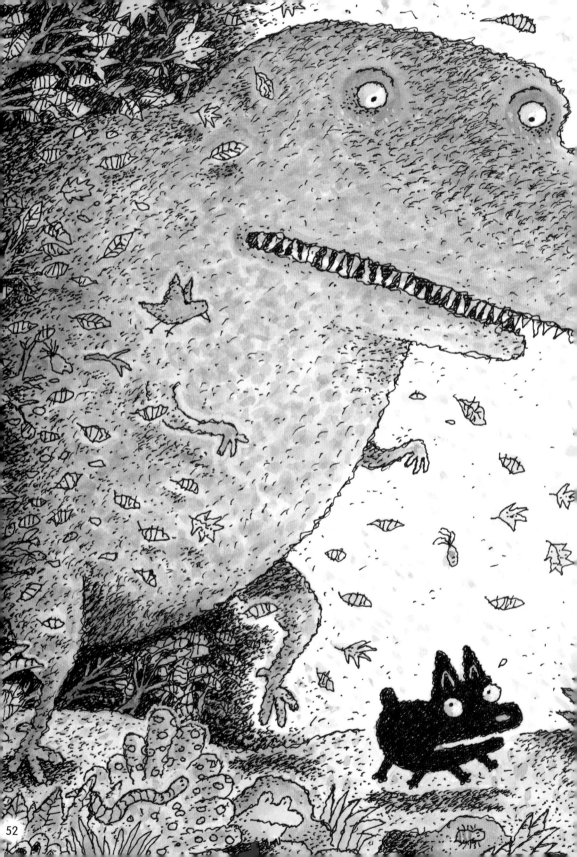

There was an old scientist who swallowed
a magnifying glass,
it was part of the mystery...

. . . of studying ancient fossils at the museum of natural history.

Fossils are evidence of life. They are the remnants of organic life from long ago. The word fossil comes from Latin *fossilis,* which means "dug up."

Fossils are formed in many ways. A **mold fossil** is when an outline or imprint is left behind but the original organism is gone. A **cast fossil** is created when an original organism deteriorates but minerals harden to create the shape of that organism. Footprints, tracks, tunnels, and even waste are **trace fossils**, which provide evidence of ancient life but are not part of an organism's actual body. Bones, teeth, exoskeletons, shells, and even leaves are **body fossils**, which are made up of actual parts of an organism.

Paleontology is the study of ancient life. A scientist who studies fossils is a **paleontologist**. By examining fossils, a paleontologist can determine what extinct animals or organisms looked like. By studying fossil remains, a scientist can estimate how the animal lived or the environment in which the organism lived.

A paleontologist uses many tools to dig up fossils. A **rock hammer** removes large pieces of rock. A **chisel** chips away tiny pieces of rock from around a fossil. A **pick** is a sharp, pointed tool that allows dirt and rock to be broken up. A **sieve** or **sifting screen** allows dirt to pass through while keeping larger chunks of rock and sediment. A **magnifying glass** gives a close-up look of tiny, hard-to-see details. Tiny brushes are used to clean out excess sediment, sand, and dirt. All the findings are kept in a notebook to record essential information.

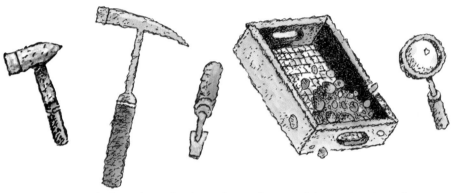

Scientists study fossils to find out how the world used to be. If an animal or plant no longer lives, it is **extinct**. Not all the dinosaurs lived at the same time. Different species were around at various times between **245 and 66 million years ago**. By looking at fossilized remains, scientists are able to learn how dinosaurs lived. For example, by studying fossilized remains and waste, they know what different types of dinosaur species ate. A dinosaur who only ate meat is a **carnivore**. One who only ate plants is a **herbivore**. Some dinosaurs were **omnivores**, which means they ate both plants and meat.

Search and Find!

Paleontologists use many different tools while they're searching and identifying fossils. Go back through the story and see if you can find all the mystery objects before the old scientist swallows them! When you've found them all, check your answers with the answer key at the bottom.

Happy searching!

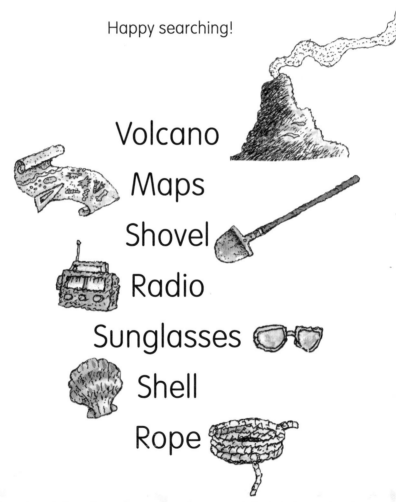

Volcano

Maps

Shovel

Radio

Sunglasses

Shell

Rope

Brush

Plastic baggie

Tape measure

Walkie-talkie

Water bottle

Safety goggles

Little rake

Flashlight

Bucket

Compass

Trowel

Camera

Notebook